*Leader's Guide
for group study of*

*What Happens
When Women
Pray*

By Evelyn Christenson

EVELYN CHRISTENSON founded United Prayer Ministry, Minneapolis, Minnesota, and spoke frequently at retreats, conventions, and seminars on the subject of prayer.

BOOKS BY EVELYN CHRISTENSON
A Study Guide for Evangelism Praying
Praying God's Way
What Happens When Women Pray
Lord, Change Me
Gaining Through Losing
What Happens When We Pray for Our Families
What Happens When God Answers Prayer
What Happens When Children Pray
Battling the Prince of Darkness
    Rescuing Captives from Satan's Kingdom

For further information visit:
www.EvelynChristensonMinistries.com

ISBN: 978-0-9817467-8-4

Prayer Is the Answer

TEXT, CHAPTER 1

Scripture

The effectual, fervent prayer of a righteous [person] availeth much. (James 5:16)

Goal

To motivate group members to pray and learn how to develop prayer power.

How to Begin

Begin the meeting with a prayer. Here is a sample that might be used, but feel free to pray your own prayer if desired.

Dear Lord, thank You that You will make Your power available to us. Help us to learn more about how we can experience that power in a more effective way in our own lives. In Jesus' name we pray, Amen.

Opening Questions
- Do you pray?
- Do you get answers to your prayers from God?
- Do you feel you are just dropping your prayers into a bottomless barrel, and nothing happens?

Introduction
If you are not satisfied with what God is doing in response to your prayers, this study is for you. In this *What Happens When Women Pray* study, we will learn more about how to have prayer power.

Group Discussion Questions
Turn to James 5:16 and John 15:7 in your Bible. Have two group members read them to the rest of the group.

1. Discuss, as you understand it, the extent of God's power as promised to us in James 5:16 and John 15:7.
2. Share with your group when (if ever) you have *felt* somebody's prayers for you.
3. Share some time when you learned that somebody felt your prayer for them, if you have had such a time.
4. Discuss whether or not you feel you are making yourself available to the prayer power promised in James 5:16.
5. If not, share some reasons why prayer usually is a last resort. For example: "I don't really know how to pray," "God never seems to answer me," "I can do it myself," "God is not interested in my little things," etc.
6. What do you think your very next step should be to gain more power in prayer? Discuss how, when, and where.

Prayer Time

Each person should pray aloud one sentence of what their heart is saying to God right now. For example, *"Lord, show me," "Lord, I'm sorry I neglected my prayer life," "Lord, cleanse me,"* or *"Lord, I want power in prayer!"*

Closing Prayer

Dear God, teach me to plug into Your power. In Jesus' name, Amen.

Assignment

1. Pray for yourself daily, thoroughly reaffirming the prayer from this lesson: *"Dear Lord, I want that power in prayer. Teach me and break me until I have it!"* Ask God to break down any inhibitions, fears, or indifference you may have.

2. Choose one prayer partner for the duration of the group study. Share only one need with your partner. Pray together, or go home promising to pray. Before your next study, call or meet with your prayer partner to exchange results, if any, from your praying for each other. If this is not possible, come a few minutes early to your group meeting and share before the session begins.

3. Practice praying about situations that arise in your normal daily life this week.

4. Read Chapter 2 for next week.

It Doesn't Take So Long

TEXT, CHAPTER 2

Scripture

If I had cherished sin in my heart, the Lord would not have listened . . . . (Psalm 66:18, NIV)

Goal

To learn Prerequisite #1 to answered prayer: no known unconfessed sin in the life of the pray-er.

How to Begin

Begin the meeting with a prayer. Here is a sample that might be used, but feel free to pray your own prayer if desired.

Dear Father, thank You for the prayer power You've promised to us. And now, today, help us to be honest and open to You as we learn the first reason why our prayers may not be as powerful as they could be. Thank You for teaching us that being an effective pray-er doesn't take long. In Jesus' name we pray, Amen.

Opening Questions

- Have you prayed daily since our last lesson? Did it get easier?
- What happened with your prayer partner? Did you actually communicate with your prayer partner? Share results if you choose.
- Have you read Chapter 2?

Introduction

In this lesson we will learn the secret of having power in our praying. Jesus said there are conditions for this power in prayer. These we will call "Prerequisites" to answered prayer. The first one will be studied in this lesson.

Discussion Questions

1. Did you have all the power you needed for your partner to feel your prayers since our last session? Is this true in most of your praying? Do you wonder why your prayers aren't always answered?
2. Review James 5:16 for the kind of person whose prayers are effective. Also see Isaiah 59:1-2 and 1 John 3:21-22.
3. What does the author mean when she says your problem may not be *"sins, but sin"*? (See Ch. 2, *A Prerequisite to Answered Prayer*.) What is the difference between "sin" (John 16:7-9a) and "sins" (1 Peter 3:12)?

Prayer Time

Go around your group, each reading one Scripture from the list of sins below and the accompanying questions.

All will pray slowly aloud with the leader, *"Lord, forgive me for . . . ."* Group members will say whatever sin they want forgiven. (Use discretion, not pride—God already knows your deepest sins, but your prayer group doesn't need to.)

After the group has finished praying through the list, the leader will ask if anyone would like to become a Christian. If you are not positive that Jesus is your Savior and Lord, He said in Mark 1:15 to repent and believe. Pray (out loud if you can) asking Jesus to come into your life as Savior and Lord.

LIST OF SCRIPTURAL SINS TO BE READ BEFORE CONFESSING SINS IN PRAYER

Every YES answer is a sin in your life that needs to be confessed. *"Therefore, he that knoweth to do good and doeth it not, to him it is sin."* (James 4:17)

1. 1 Thessalonians 5:18
   "In everything give thanks; for this is the will of God in Christ Jesus concerning you."

   Do you worry about anything? Have you failed to thank God for all things, the seemingly bad as well as the good? Do you neglect to give thanks at mealtimes?

2. Ephesians 3:20
   "Now unto him who is able to do exceedingly abundantly above all that we ask or think, according to the power that worketh in us . . . ."

   Do you fail to attempt things for God because you are not talented enough? Do feelings of inferiority keep you from trying to serve God? When you do accomplish something for Christ, do you fail to give Him all the glory?

3. Acts 1:8

"But ye shall receive power, after the Holy Spirit is come upon you; and ye shall be witnesses unto me both in Jerusalem, and in all Judea, and in Samaria, and unto the uttermost part of the earth."

Have you failed to be a witness for Christ with your life? Have you felt it was enough just to live your Christianity and not witness with your mouth to the lost?

4. Romans 12:3

"For I say . . . to every man that is among you, not to think of himself more highly than he ought to think . . . ."

Are you proud of your accomplishments, your talents, your family? Do you fail to see others as better, more important than yourself in the body of Christ? Do you insist on your own rights? Do you think as a Christian you are doing quite well?

5. Ephesians 4:31

"Let all bitterness, and wrath, and anger, and clamor, and evil speaking, be put away from you, with all malice."

Do you complain, find fault, argue? Do you have a critical spirit? Do you carry a grudge against Christians of another group because they don't see eye-to-eye with you on all things? Do you speak unkindly about people when they are not present? Are you angry with yourself? With others? With God?

6. 1 Corinthians 6:19
    "What? Know ye not that your body is the temple of the Holy Spirit who is in you, whom ye have of God, and ye are not your own?"

    Are you careless with your body? Are you guilty of not caring for it as the temple of the Holy Spirit in eating and exercise habits?

7. Ephesians 4:29
    "Let no corrupt communication proceed out of your mouth . . . ."

    Do you ever use filthy language, tell slightly off-color jokes? Do you condone others doing so in your presence, in your home?

8. Ephesians 4:27
    "Neither give place to the devil."

    Do you fail to see you are a "landing strip" for Satan when you open your mind to him through transcendental meditation, yoga, séances, psychic predictions, occult literature, Satanic music, movies, TV, websites, pornography, and pornographic literature? Do you get advice for daily living from horoscopes rather than from God? Do you let Satan use you to thwart the cause of Christ in your church through criticism, gossip, and lack of support?

9. Romans 12:11

"[Be] not slothful in business . . . ."

Do you fail to pay your debts on time? Avoid paying them altogether? Do you charge more on credit cards than you can pay when due? Do you neglect to keep honest income tax records? Do you engage in any shady business deals whether as an employer or employee?

10. 1 Corinthians 8:9

"But take heed lest by any means the liberty of yours become a stumbling block to them that are weak."

Do you feel you can do anything you want to do because the Bible says you are free in Christ? Even though you were strong enough not to fall, do you fail to take responsibility for a weaker Christian who has fallen because of following your example?

11. Hebrews 10:25

"Not forsaking the assembling of ourselves together . . . ."

Are you irregular or sporadic in church attendance? Do you attend preaching services in body only, whispering, reading or planning while God's Word is being preached? Are you skipping prayer meetings? Have you neglected family devotions?

12. Colossians 3:9

"Lie not to one another, seeing that ye have put off the old man and his deeds . . . ."

Do you ever lie? Exaggerate? Do you fail to see "little white lies" as sin? Do you tell things the way you want them rather than the way they really are?

13. 1 Peter 2:11
"Dearly beloved . . . abstain from fleshly lusts which war against the soul."

Are you guilty of a lustful eye toward the opposite sex? Do you fill your mind with sexually oriented TV programs, movies, books, magazines? Their covers? Centerfolds? Do you indulge in any lustful activity God's Word condemns—fornication, adultery, perversion?

14. John 13:35
"By this shall all men know that ye are my disciples, if ye have love one to another."

Are you guilty of being a part of factions and divisions in your church? Would you rather add fuel to a misunderstanding than help correct it? Have you loved only the ones in your own church, feeling those of other denominations are not of the body of Christ? Are you secretly pleased over the misfortunes of another? Annoyed by their successes?

15. Colossians 3:13
"Forbearing one another, and forgiving one another, if any man have a quarrel against any; even as Christ forgave you, so also do ye."

Have you failed to forgive anybody anything he or she might have said or done against you? Have you chosen to ignore certain people? Are you holding a grudge?

16. Ephesians 4:28

    "Let him that stole steal no more: but rather let him labor . . . ."

    Do you steal from your employer by doing less work, staying on the job less time than you are paid for? Do you underpay?

17. Ephesians 5:16

    "Redeeming the time, because the days are evil."

    Do you waste your time? The time of others? Do you spend time watching unprofitable TV, reading cheap books, procrastinating?

18. Matthew 6:24

    "No man can serve two masters . . . . Ye cannot serve God and [money]."

    Is your goal in life to make as much money as possible? Accumulate things? Have you withheld God's share of your income from Him? Is money your god?

19. Matthew 23:28

    "Even so ye outwardly appear righteous unto men, but within ye are full of hypocrisy and iniquity."

    Do you know in your heart you are a fake, just pretending to be a real Christian? Are you hiding behind church membership to cover a life still full of sin? Are you faking Christianity for social status, acceptance in your church, community? Do you smile piously during the Sunday sermon but live in your sin all week? Are you the person at home that you claim to be?

20. Philippians 4:8
"Finally, brethren, whatsoever things are true, whatsoever things are honest, whatsoever things are just, whatsoever things are pure, whatsoever things are lovely, whatsoever things are of good report; if there be any virtue, and if there be any praise, think on these things."

Do you enjoy listening to gossip? Passing it on? Do you believe rumors or partial truths, especially about an enemy or your competitor? Do you fail to spend time every day reading the Bible? Do you fail to think on the things of God—only good and true and pure things—always?

Closing Prayer
Dear Lord, thank You that You have forgiven the sin or sins we have confessed.

Thank You, Lord, for cleansing me as You promised in 1 John 1:9 and qualifying me for effectual, intercessory prayer. In Jesus' name, Amen.

Assignment
1. At home, reread your list of Scriptural Sins, confessing any God brings to your attention as still a sin in your life. (Leader: permission is granted to make and distribute copies of the Scriptural Sins to your group.)
2. If you accepted Christ today or made sure He was your personal Savior and Lord, share it with an appropriate person (someone in your group, the group leader, your minister, a Christian friend) immediately. Be sure to start reading your Bible every day and going to church.

3. Pray together with your prayer partner again before your next meeting.
4. Read Chapter 3 for next week.

Forgiven as We Forgive

TEXT, CHAPTER 3

Scripture
Forgive our sins, just as we have forgiven those who have sinned against us. (Matthew 6:12, TLB)

Goal
To learn Prerequisite #2 to answered prayer: to have right relationships with other people as well as with God. "Forgiven *as* we forgive."

How to Begin
Begin the meeting with a prayer. Here is a sample that might be used, but feel free to pray your own prayer if desired.

Dear Father, thank You that You forgave as we confessed our sins to You. Help us to see that there is a condition to Your forgiving: that we forgive other people. Lord, this is a hard lesson that You taught us. In Jesus' name, Amen.

Opening Questions

- After reading through the list of sins this week, did you find more areas for confession?
- Have you read Chapter 3?

Introduction

In this lesson we will examine a startling condition Jesus told us about that is a key to powerful prayer. This "key" opens the door to God's forgiving the sins of Christians. If we don't forgive others, Jesus said God won't forgive our sins either and won't answer our prayers.

Discussion Questions

1. Were you surprised to find that there are conditions to God forgiving sins? (Important: God has no condition for when we repent and ask Jesus Christ to be our Savior, forgiving that state of sin into which we all were born. These instructions are written to Christians only. It is *after* we become Christians that God requires us to forgive other people.)
2. Turn to Matthew 6:12, 14-15 and Mark 11:24-25. Ask a different person in your group to read each passage with the following question in mind: What condition is attached to Christians being forgiven by God for sins committed after accepting Jesus?
3. Discuss several meanings of the word "as" and then put them into the whole sentence of Matthew 6:12.
4. If you were still lacking in prayer power after confessing your sins last session, what reason might be responsible for this, in light of the previous questions and Scriptures?

5. Turn to 2 Corinthians 2:5-11. Ask someone in the group to read it aloud. Discuss God's steps in the "forgiving" formula of this passage.

Prayer Time

1. Silently ask God to bring to your mind one person who has grieved you and whom you have not completely forgiven.
2. Now, forgive that person in silent prayer, asking God to give you the strength and ability if you need to.
3. Aloud, all together, ask God to forgive you for the sin of not forgiving that person. Do NOT mention the name of the person. (Now that you have forgiven others, God also has forgiven those sins you and your fellow Christians have confessed. Now God will hear you Christians, including those who accepted Jesus Christ in our last lesson.)
4. Now, all together out loud, ask God for as much love as He wants you to have for the person who grieved you. Wait in silence a minute, giving God time to answer.
5. Next, all together out loud, ask God how you should confirm your love to that person. Wait in silence for thoughts He puts in your mind.
6. Pray, promising God that you will do whatever He has told you and will tell you.

Closing Prayer

Dear Lord, thank You that as I forgave, You forgave sins I have confessed. Help me to obey what You have told me to do. In Jesus' name, Amen.

Assignment

1. Do what you promised God in your prayer time, using discretion.
2. Read Chapter 4 for next week.

Praying in One Accord

TEXT, CHAPTER 4

Scripture

These all continued with one accord in prayer and supplication, with the women, and Mary the mother of Jesus, and with His brethren. (Acts 1:14)

Goal

To realize the thrill and power of praying with members of the body of Christ, including men, women, and children.

How to Begin

Begin the meeting with a prayer. Here is a sample that might be used, but feel free to pray your own prayer if desired.

Dear Father, thank You that we have the privilege of the whole body of Christ praying together. Show us Your answers from the Bible that will break down any prejudices we may have. Give us newfound joy today. In Jesus' name, Amen.

Opening Questions
- Would anyone like to share how they followed up with the person they forgave last week? What were the results? (If needed, have a short prayer time for the situation.)
- Have you read Chapter 4?

Introduction
In this lesson we will be learning how to join forces with other people in experiencing power through our praying.

Discussion Questions
1. Read Acts 1:14. When Jesus left the earth and ascended back into heaven, what did His followers immediately do? How did this fulfill Jesus' prayer for unity in John 17:23?
2. What occurs to you from Acts 1:14 regarding with whom you too can pray? Discuss any prejudices or barriers your church or you have personally to what the Bible says.
3. Instead of suffering from "paralysis of analysis" (see Ch. 4, *Changes*), how should we approach problems?
4. Think of at least one situation in which you might implement the "pray first and plan afterward" program. Discuss some specific ways you could encourage or actually start corporate praying in your church, Sunday School class, organization, committees, neighborhood, home.

Prayer Time

Have no more than four people per prayer group. As time permits, take turns having one person pray about a prayer request while the rest of the group prays silently, in one accord, on the same subject. Recognize Jesus' presence.

Closing Prayer

Father, teach me to pray in one accord with other people with Jesus in our midst, sharing their burdens, joys, and petitions. In Jesus' name, Amen.

Assignment

1. Begin to encourage corporate praying (pray first and plan afterward) in at least one organization in which you are involved.
2. Broaden your understanding of what the prayer movement in your city is doing.
3. Read Chapter 5 for next week.

The Six S's Method

TEXT, CHAPTER 5

Scripture

And when you pray, do not keep on babbling like pagans, for they think they will be heard because of their many words. Do not be like them, for your Father knows what you need before you ask him. (Matthew 6:7-8, NIV)

Goal

To learn and practice a simple yet profound method of praying that is effective for beginners through mature pray-ers.

How to Begin

Begin the meeting with a prayer. Here is a sample that might be used, but feel free to pray your own prayer if desired.

Dear Father, thank You for showing us the power and joy of praying in one accord. Now today, Lord, show us specifically how to do it. Father, give courage to those who have not yet learned to pray and joy to the mature pray-ers as they all learn to pray together. In Jesus' name, Amen.

Opening Questions
- Share any opportunities and progress made in starting a prayer group for your community, school, etc.
- Have you read Chapter 5?

Introduction
In this lesson we will study a method of intercessory prayer—the small-group Six S method. If new people do not come to your small prayer groups or if they come but don't participate as much as you do, then there will be help for you in these instructions.

Discussion Questions
Try to find the answer to any problems you might be having in your present prayer group in the following Six S rules. (The secret is starting by putting ourselves on the level of the most inexperienced pray-er in the group.)

"S" #1: Subject by Subject
1. When praying for just one subject at a time, how is it possible for all to pray silently in one accord with or for the person praying audibly?
2. Is planning your own long prayer in advance ever a problem for you? Explain. Does this help new Christians and inexperienced pray-ers feel comfortable or thwart their praying with you?

"S" #2: Short Prayers
1. What two things did Jesus say about long, repetitive prayers in Matthew 6:7-8?

24

2. Consider the possibility that those who are eager to learn to pray might be intimidated by long prayers they haven't mastered yet. What do you think new members might feel about their importance to God when you take up almost all the time with your praying?

3. When do you think it is appropriate to pray long prayers?

"S" #3: Simple Prayers

1. Are you discouraging new Christians and inexperienced pray-ers from praying with you because of your high-sounding language that they can't use yet?

2. Are you feeling spiritually superior because you keep coming to prayer meetings and they don't? What are some possible reasons that they are not coming to your prayer meetings?

3. Are you willing to bring yourself down to the level of the least mature pray-er coming into your group—to see growth in numbers and the amount of participation?

"S" #4: Specific Requests/Answers Recorded and Dated

1. Do you fail to recognize something as God's answer because you forgot you prayed? How can keeping a notebook solve this problem?

2. Does your prayer group immediately start asking God for something before taking time to thank and praise Him for what He has already done in answer to previous praying? Keeping track of requests and answers is the source of your praising and thanking.

Could this be the cause for lack of interest in continued praying?

3. If you keep track of dates and answers to prayer, discuss how this has helped you mature spiritually: what and when God answers teaches us how, when, and why God answers. How will keeping track of your requests and answers help you know how to pray next time?

"S" #5: Silent Periods

1. Why is it important to God for us to have silent time between prayers at a small-group prayer meeting?
2. Do you become uncomfortable when someone isn't praying aloud in your group? How do you fill the silence?
3. Discuss our talking *at* God vs. listening *to* Him. Do you think God ever gets frustrated at our one-sided conversations? What are we missing?

"S" #6: Small Groups

1. Have you experienced that you are not intimidated and pray more frankly and frequently in a small group vs. a large group? Why?
2. How does Jesus' promise in Matthew 18:20 make your small group a rare privilege?

Prayer Time

Have you said before that you cannot pray aloud? Give it a try! Make groups of no more than four. Quickly review the Six S rules. Have each group decide on a list of prayer requests. The leader will announce the first request. Take turns each praying audibly on that request, strictly adhering to the Six S rules. When all who choose to pray have finished, the leader will give the next prayer request. Repeat the process.

Closing Prayer

Dear Father, please give me the privilege of being aware of the presence of Jesus, my Savior, in a prayer group. Teach me to help others to pray. In Jesus' name, Amen.

Assignment

1. Introduce the Six S way of praying to everyone in your home, including your youngest child or roommate, giving every member of your household equal prayer time. Let your children "take turns praying." Be an example in any prayer group you may be in.
2. Read Chapter 6 for next week.

How to Pray in God's Will

TEXT, CHAPTER 6

Scripture

This is the confidence we have in approaching God: that if we ask anything according to his will, he hears us. And if we know that he hears us—whatever we ask—we know that we have what we asked of him. (1 John 5:14-15, NIV)

Goal

To learn Prerequisite #3A to answered prayer: praying in God's will.

How to Begin

Begin the meeting with a prayer. Here is a sample that might be used, but feel free to pray your own prayer if desired.

Dear Lord, thank You for showing us such a simple "Six S" prayer method that works in such awesome ways. Now we are ready for another prerequisite—praying in Your will. How hard this seems, Father, and yet it is the precious key to assurance of answered prayer. In Jesus' name, Amen.

Opening Questions

- Share experiences of the "Six S" method in your home, church, etc. In this short time, did you notice any positive changes?
- Have you read Chapter 6?

Introduction

This week, we will learn another condition for God answering prayer: Prerequisite #3A, praying in God's will.

Discussion Questions

1. Turn to the Lord's model prayer in Matthew 6:9-13. Ask one group member to read it aloud. Is there anything contrary to God's will in heaven?
2. Discuss why you are hesitant to pray God's will.
3. Discuss what would happen if every Christian brought God's will into their sphere of influence: in our homes, cities, churches, and nations.
4. Think of one specific prayer you prayed recently that you could discuss with your group to see if it was God's will or your will.
5. Turn to 1 John 5:14-15. Have one group member read it aloud as the others listen. Review the seeming paradox of praying *God's* will and what *we* desire in 1 John 5:14-15. In the past, with which one were you most comfortable? Why?
6. Read Luke 22:39-44. What did the Lord Jesus ask His Father? Why do you think the Holy Spirit had this soul struggle of the Lord Jesus recorded for us? Reread this passage aloud with this question in mind:

How did Jesus' word "nevertheless" or "yet" in Gethsemane solve this paradox? What changed—the words of His prayer or His attitude—that made the difference?

7. What insights have you gained about the fact that God has closed some doors to you in the past? Could this have been because of your insisting on what you wanted? What doors has He opened?

8. What would be the potential of us bringing our wills into conformity with God's will? See Luke 1:26-38. Like Mary, how does this enable God to open awesome doors for us too?

Prayer Time

Lead group members in the prayer below, reading each sentence and then pausing for them to repeat aloud, if they mean it.

Dear Father in heaven . . . (Group repeats)

I want only Your will in my life . . . (Group repeats)

Open the doors You have for me . . . (Group repeats)

Give me the faith in who You are . . . (Group repeats)

And the courage I need to go through them . . . (Group repeats)

Thank you, Lord . . . *Amen.* (Group repeats)

Closing Prayer

Lord, we truly want Your will in our lives and in our spheres of influence. Thank You in advance for the open doors you have for us. In Jesus' name, Amen.

Assignment

1. Honestly pray God's will in some decision you must make this week.

2. If you haven't already, begin a disciplined reading and study of God's Word, the Bible, to see who He really is.
3. Continue to share prayer requests with your prayer partner, practicing wanting God's will for each.
4. Read Chapter 7 for next week.

God Never Makes a Mistake

TEXT, CHAPTER 7

Scripture

Wherefore let them that suffer according to the will of God commit the keeping of their souls to him in well doing, as unto a faithful Creator. (1 Peter 4:19)

Goal

To learn Prerequisite #3B: God is a loving, omniscient Father to whom we can pray with perfect confidence, knowing that God's answer will be for our good and the good of those for whom we are praying.

How to Begin

Begin the meeting with a prayer. Here is a sample that might be used, but feel free to pray your own prayer if desired.

Dear Lord, thank You for teaching us how to be like Jesus in conforming our wills to Yours. Help us today to learn to pray with perfect confidence in Your will because of who You are. In Jesus' name, Amen.

Opening Questions
- As you tried to "live" the last lesson (praying in God's will), did you find it difficult or easy?
- Have you read Chapter 7?

Introduction
Our session last week covered the first half of Prerequisite #3, "Praying in God's Will." This session will cover the second half, "God Never Makes a Mistake." We will learn that Jesus not only taught God's will with His words, but lived it with His life; and, in doing so, solved the seeming paradox of what God wills and what we want. We will also learn how applying this in our lives will produce great prayer power.

Discussion Questions
1. Share how you feel God has made mistakes in your life. Why do you consider these things mistakes?
2. Does the fact that God is all-knowing and never makes a mistake change your answer to the first question? How?
3. Read Romans 8:28. What might be God's reason? God may show us many of His reasons, but some not until eternity.
4. How would your view of God's omniscience (all-knowingness, including the future) change you from praying answers to praying requests to God? Read James 4:3. How does God answering "no" because He knows the "what ifs" keep us from falling on our faces?

5. How and why can it be God's will for us to suffer? Apply it personally if possible.
6. Read Philippians 4:6-7. According to these verses, what should we include with our requests—even before God answers the way He chooses? Why? Apply this concept to something you are praying for.

Prayer Time

1. Silently think of the most important thing in the world to you. (It may be health, a loved one, a job, finances, schooling, etc.)
2. Now silently pray; *Father, I give You [name] that is most important in the world to me.*
3. Now, audibly all together, thank God in advance for however He will choose to answer, knowing it will be according to His perfect, all-knowing will.
4. (Please don't pray the following prayer unless you really mean it.) All together: *Father, I want Your will in every area of my life including my job, my home, my health, my children, my loved ones, my spouse, and my service for You. In Jesus' name, Amen.*

Closing Prayer

Father, thank You that all of us who prayed this prayer have now brought ourselves into conformity with Your will—and will receive what we want, because now we only want what You want—Your will. In Jesus' name, Amen.

Assignment

1. Spend as much time alone in prayer as it takes to thoroughly settle in your heart the prayers of today's prayer time.
2. Practice thanking God, before He answers, for whatever He chooses to do with the material

possessions, circumstances, and people you gave Him today.

3. Be willing to accept God's open—and closed—doors as they come into your life. Praise Him for both.
4. Continue to meet with your prayer partner to pray together, helping each other discern God's will and His possible reasons.
5. Read Chapter 8 for next week.

The Space Dimension of Prayer — Where We Pray

TEXT, CHAPTER 8

Scripture

But thou, when thou prayest, enter into thy closet, and when thou hast shut thy door, pray to thy Father which is in secret; and thy Father which seeth in secret shall reward thee openly. (Matthew 6:6)

Goal

To learn Prerequisite #4A to effective prayer: the importance of a daily closet prayer time and the privilege of praying in any posture.

How to Begin

Begin the meeting with a prayer. Here is a sample that might be used, but feel free to pray your own prayer if desired.

Dear God, thank You that as the hard things came this week, we could relax in Your never making a mistake. And now, Lord, we're excited to learn the secret of the most vital type of praying we can do. In Jesus' name, Amen.

Opening Questions

- Did anyone find a circumstance in which you could not pray for God's will?
- Would anyone share a difficult situation that you have been praying for God to remove, but now you actually thank God for—because He never makes a mistake?
- Did God surprise any of you by not answering the way you expected?
- Have you read Chapter 8?

Introduction

In this lesson we will learn why having a daily closet prayer time is an important prerequisite to power in prayer.

Discussion Questions

1. What are some reasons for calling daily closet prayer time a prerequisite to prayer power?
2. Share if you have a special, holy spot where you meet God in a special way.
3. How does having a daily prayer closet influence power in short or public prayers? Discuss this statement: "The quality (power) of your short, public prayers is determined by the quality and quantity of your closet praying."
4. How much power do you really want in prayer? How does the amount of time you spend in your prayer closet influence the amount of power? Encourage each other by sharing the joy, wisdom,

and communion with God you have experienced in your personal prayer closet.

5. However, does it matter to God where we are when we pray or what position we assume? Have each group member look up and tell the different biblical places and postures mentioned in the following verses: Luke 22:41; John 11:41; Matthew 26:39; Mark 11:25; Numbers 16:22; 2 Chronicles 7:1-3; Psalm 134:2; 1 Timothy 2:8; Psalm 4:4; Daniel 6:10; 1 Kings 19:4.

6. Are you judgmental of people whose posture in prayer differs from your customary one? Is your prayer posture really a scriptural one? Would you be willing to try another scriptural posture?

7. Share any unusual postures or places you have prayed. How do you think your need and kind of praying dictated the posture you assumed? (Were you feeling guilty, submissive, filled with praise, adoring, etc.?)

Prayer Time

1. Have a time of silent prayer, praying about where God wants your prayer closet to be in your house. Ask God to show you your responsibility of making a holy place with Him.

2. In silence (remembering that prayer is a two-way conversation), wait for God to bring thoughts to your mind.

3. Promise God you will do it immediately.

4. Ask God to forgive you for judging those who pray differently than you do, especially if their posture is more scriptural than yours.

Closing Prayer

Lord, give us the joy of secret closet praying. Keep us faithful to shut the door every day and spend time with You and Your Word in secret. Teach us to draw apart alone with You, no matter where we are or with whom. In Jesus' name, Amen.

Assignment

1. If you have not already established a place for your closet praying, pick one that will be as private as possible and conducive to spending time alone with God.
2. Set the time for your closet prayer. Ask God to help you keep it faithfully.
3. Suggested prayers to include in your praying:
   - Draw near to your holy God.
   - Confess any known sin.
   - Praise, worship, adore, and thank Him.
   - Ask God to search your heart for any unrecognized sin, and then confess it.
   - Ask God to fill you with Himself—the Holy Spirit, Son, and Father.
   - Forgive all who have hurt you by word or deed.
   - Submit to God's will for your life that day—and any decision affecting the future.
   - Accept the circumstances that you can't change, asking God to change you in them.
   - Claim victory over Satan.
   - Exchange your mutual love with God.
   - Listen to God. Jot down what He tells you in your notebook.
   - Wait in His presence for your dwindling mental, emotional, physical, and spiritual resources to be replenished.

- Intercede for others—especially the non-Christians you know.
4. Be sure to meet with your prayer partner.
5. Read Chapter 9 for next week.

The Time Dimension of Prayer — When We Pray

TEXT, CHAPTER 9

Scripture

Pray without ceasing. (1 Thessalonians 5:17)

Goal

To learn Prerequisite #4B to answered prayer: to understand the possibility of always being tuned in to God and, as a result, learning to "pray without ceasing."

How to Begin

Begin the meeting with a prayer. Here is a sample that might be used, but feel free to pray your own prayer if desired.

Dear Lord, thank You for the precious experiences we've had with You this week, talking with You in our prayer closets. Now this week, show us the awesome possibilities of praying even when we aren't in our prayer closets. In Jesus' name, Amen.

Opening Questions
- Did any of you establish a closet prayer time for the first time this week? Share your experience.
- Did you try any new postures in prayer this week? How did it affect your prayer life?
- Have you read Chapter 9?

Introduction
In our last study, we talked about the importance of having a daily closet prayer time. Today, we will learn what to do *after* we finish our daily closet prayer time.

Discussion Questions
1. What do the phrases "pray without ceasing" (1 Thessalonians 5:17), "pray always" (Ephesians 6:18), and "pray everywhere" (1 Timothy 2:8) mean to you? How can you obey these commands?
2. Are you a lark or an owl? How does it affect your prayer life?
3. With which do you identify: keeping the prayer door open when finishing your closet praying, or slamming the door on God, feeling you have given Him all He requires? Take time to honestly think this through and share with your group.
4. Since none of us can be a monk in a closet all day and must put our minds to other things, how can we realistically pray without ceasing? Share how you pray without ceasing.
5. For whose benefit are we to keep our communication system open with God 24 hours a day, i.e., praying without ceasing—ours, God's, others', or all three?
6. What changes will you have to make in your attitudes and priorities in order to be available to

others and Him 24 hours a day? What is the difference between talking "at" God and just being open to Him all day? Discuss honestly.

7. In our last study, we discussed the postures of prayer. Since any posture in which we can't include God is sin, are there places you found yourself last week where you could not have your communication system open to Him?

Prayer Time

1. Draw close to God.
2. In silence, take time to mentally run through your phone calls, workplace contacts, TV watching, movies, life in your home, school, etc.
3. Praying aloud if possible, ask God to forgive you for any posture or place where you couldn't include Him.
4. Ask God to forgive you for "slamming the door" by not praying all through the day, and not being available at night.
5. Ask God to make you spiritually sensitive to every need (i.e., newspapers, neighbors, TV, family) you see and immediately send an SOS prayer.
6. Ask God to help you have enough faith to pray, knowing that although you may not be able to help in the situation, God in His omnipotence can.

Closing Prayer

Dear Father, I want to be available to You, 24 hours a day. Teach me to open my communication with You and never shut it. Also help me to be available to others whenever they need me to pray. In Jesus' name, Amen.

Assignment

1. Practice keeping your communication system open with God 24 hours a day so that you can get through to Him immediately with your SOS prayers.
2. Before retiring tonight, reaffirm to God that you are available to Him all night. Give Him your night, trusting Him to decide how much sleep you need.
3. As opportunities present themselves, let others (family, friends, colleagues at work or school, church members, pastor) know that you are available to pray for them if they have a need. Search out one person who has a visible need, and, as God leads, assure that person you will pray. But be sure to pray. (It helps to pray immediately.)
4. Practice using scriptural postures of prayer other than your usual ones. Keep alert as you read the Bible, and note any new ones that come up.
5. Meet with your prayer partner. Promise each other to be available 24 hours a day to pray for the other. If possible, and with discretion, inform those for whom you are praying that you would love to pray for them if they ever want to tell you of a need that has arisen in their lives. If no natural opportunity arises, trust God's timing and merely report this back to your group.
6. Read Chapter 10 for next week.

The Vertical Dimension of Prayer — To Whom We Pray

TEXT, CHAPTER 10

Scripture

Submit yourselves, then, to God. Resist the devil, and he will flee from you. Come near to God and he will come near to you. (James 4:7-8, NIV)

Goal

To learn Prerequisite #5: to make sure it is God in heaven to whom we draw close, and to be alert to Satan's interfering and hindering.

How to Begin

Begin the meeting with a prayer. Here is a sample that might be used, but feel free to pray your own prayer if desired.

Thank You, Lord, that You not only expect us to stay open to You 24 hours a day, but You are delighted when we do. Thank You for the precious experiences You've given us this week. Now teach us a biblical warning about opening our minds to the supernatural. In Jesus' name, Amen.

Opening Questions

- Did God wake any of you in the night, either since our last lesson or sometime before it, to pray for someone He knew had a need? Share very briefly.
- Share any scriptural postures of prayer you tried that were new to you.
- Report on any interaction with those for whom you are praying. Did any of you find an opportunity to tell someone for whom you've been praying that you would pray for him or her if a need arose? (If any find Christ, be sure to invite that person to your church, prayer meeting, this study, etc.)
- Have you read Chapter 10?

Introduction

This is the only prerequisite that will deal with an unpleasant subject. Because it seems negative, we frequently skip the biblical teaching about it. But Jesus did not. One fourth of His recorded ministry deals with this subject. So we will be studying not only Jesus' words in this lesson, but also the words the Holy Spirit inspired Jesus' half-brother, James, to write. However, you will actually find this a very victorious subject, and that complying with this prerequisite will change your prayer life.

Discussion Questions

1. Have one person read James 4:7-8 aloud. Discuss this question: What (1) command and (2) promise do we find in James 4:7-8 about *each* of the only two supernatural powers in the universe?

2. Have you been turning these two commands around— resisting God and drawing close to Satan— by becoming involved in pagan meditations, New Age dabbling, demonic music, occult games and videos, horoscopes, etc.? Read Deuteronomy 18:9-14 in a modern translation. What are people who do these things? How will these things keep you from drawing near to God?

3. Discuss what resisting the devil in James 4:7 means to you in a practical way.

4. Turn to 1 John 3:8 and John 19:30. Have a different person in each small group read each verse as the group listens with this question in mind: How do we know we have absolute victory in Jesus? Claim 1 John 4:4. Read Revelation 12:9-11.

5. Turn to Colossians 1:16 and Matthew 16:16. Have two people read one verse each, as the group listens with this question in mind: Was Jesus also Lord before the cross and His resurrection?

6. Turn to John 17:15 and Hebrews 7:25. Ask different group members to read each verse aloud. Then discuss these questions: What did Jesus pray for His followers and those who would teach us? (John 17:15) Now that He is making intercession for us in heaven (Hebrews 7:25), do you think He is still praying that for us? Why?

7. Since Jesus said, "No man cometh to the Father but by me" (John 14:6), is there any way you need to change your thinking about pagan religions and non-Christian praying? How?

8. Since Satan's goal is to defeat Christian leaders, how much and what kind of prayer should we be praying

for our leaders? Read 1 Peter 5:8, 1 Thessalonians 2:8, and 2 Thessalonians 3:3.

Prayer Time

1. Before starting to pray, in absolute silence practice drawing close to God. This may involve confessing some sin that God brings to your mind. If so, confess it, so that there is nothing between you and God in heaven.
2. Now draw close to Him. Wait in silence until you feel God is there.
3. Each pray one sentence of praise as to who God is.
4. Confess any occult involvement.
5. Ask God to help you recognize any thoughts or attitudes that are NOT consistent with Scripture, and thus cannot be from God.
6. Pray, claiming the blood of Jesus in His name over any of these things that are not of God.
7. Praise God for the victory in Jesus.

Closing Prayer

Thank You, Father, for the two promises. We're absolutely trusting in Jesus' victory over Satan and are so grateful for Your promise that You will draw close to us when we draw close to You. In Jesus' name, Amen.

Assignment

1. In your daily private praying, thank and praise God for your victory in Jesus over Satan. Learn to claim the name and blood of Jesus over your church, members of your family, and your own life.
2. Practice claiming the blood of Jesus over the non-Christians you are praying for, emphatically telling Satan that Jesus died for each one of them and he has

no right to hinder them from accepting Jesus as Savior and Lord. Spend time praising and thanking Jesus for willingly paying the price to defeat Satan on the cross.

3. Read Chapter 11 for next week.

The Horizontal Dimension of Prayer – Results

TEXT, CHAPTER 11

Scripture

But without faith it is impossible to please him: for he that cometh to God must believe that he is, and that he is a rewarder of them that diligently seek him. (Hebrews 11:6)

Goal

To learn Prerequisite #6 to answered prayer: to find the visible results of intercessory prayer here on earth, to discover that God is a rewarder of those who seek Him in prayer, and to see that the reason for all the prerequisites is to produce prayers with power.

How to Begin

Begin the meeting with a prayer. Here is a sample that might be used, but feel free to pray your own prayer if desired.

Thank You, Lord, that when it really is You to whom we draw close in prayer, You really do answer. Show us today the awesomeness of the fact that You reward our praying with Your divine answers. In Jesus' name, Amen.

Opening Questions

- Would someone share about their experience of resisting Satan? For instance, did you obey the biblical command to resist Satan in your own life and in prayer for others? Or did you find it difficult or seemingly unnecessary to resist Satan in prayer?
- Has anyone begun to experience the promise in James 4:7 that if you do resist, Satan will flee from you?
- Have you read Chapter 11?

Introduction

This lesson may not seem like a prerequisite to prayer power to you, but it is an extremely important one. As we study intercessory prayer, you will see that learning and obeying all the other conditions for prayer power still will not produce power—*unless there is actual praying.* The results we humans see represent the horizontal dimension of prayer. In light of this, we will treat it as Prerequisite #6.

Discussion Questions

1. Do you remember the prerequisites to powerful prayer we have studied so far? They are:
   #1: No known unconfessed sin in the life of the pray-er (Chapter 2)
   #2: Forgiven as we forgive (Chapter 3)
   #3: Praying in God's will (Chapters 6 and 7)
   #4: Personal prayer life of the pray-er (Chapters 8 and 9)

#5: Make sure it is God to whom we have drawn near (Chapter 10)

#6: Intercessory prayer (Chapters 11 and 12)

Today, we will learn Prerequisite #6 to effective prayer: seeing the results of God's answers when we pray for others in intercession. The pray-er must not only believe who God is, but also that He is a rewarder of them that diligently seek Him.

2. The Father has given the role of intercessor to three persons—His Son Jesus (Hebrews 7:25), His Holy Spirit (Romans 8:26-27), and you (1 Timothy 2:1). Look up these verses and find the three intercessors. Keeping this in mind, what awesome company does this put you in when you pray? How much of this privilege are you missing?

3. Turn to James 4:2b and ask a member of your group to read it aloud. Discuss why asking in intercession is a prerequisite to prayer power.

4. Analyze the prayer requests of your group to see how you are progressing in adding spiritual needs in addition to just physical needs.

5. Is there some great pray-er you knew who has gone to heaven (parent, pastor, Sunday School teacher), and is no longer praying here on earth? If so, *briefly* tell that person's name and relationship to you. Consider and discuss the possibility that God may want you to pick up that person's mantle of prayer.

6. Think of the organizations, church, Sunday School, etc. where you are involved that would benefit from some special method of intercessory prayer we have studied (prayer partners, a prayer calendar, prayer

letters, 24-hour clock, triplets, etc.). Discuss ways you can encourage or help start them.

7. Are there those who are separated from you with whom you need to learn a unity in prayer? Discuss some specific person. (Philippians 1:3-4)

Prayer Time

1. Thank God for His entrusting us with the awesome privilege of the same job He gave to His Son and the Holy Spirit.
2. Ask God to forgive you for letting Him down by not using all the potential power in prayer He has given You.
3. Ask God to give you the next specific step He has for you in prayer—a group He wants you to join or start, or a new method of prayer for your church, group, family, or club.
4. Wait in silence for Him to speak.
5. Aloud, promise Him you will start immediately whatever He is telling you to do.

Closing Prayer

Dear Lord, we're standing in awe that You let us help You run the earth by praying, and that You change people and situations by Your answers to our prayers. In Jesus' name, Amen.

Assignment

1. Include more specific intercessory prayer in your daily closet praying.
2. If you are married, do everything possible to begin to have meaningful prayer with your spouse. If not married, or in addition to your spouse, find one prayer partner of your own sex with whom you can

share your deep prayer needs, and for whom you can provide the same support.

3. Continue your intercessory prayer for non-Christians. Contact as many as possible to find out their immediate needs for your praying. Keep praying for them to find Christ as Savior and Lord, as long as it takes.

4. Choose one new method of intercessory prayer you will try to get started as soon as possible. Make the necessary contacts to begin.

5. Read Chapter 12 and bring your prayer notebook to next week's session.

Telephone Prayer Chains

TEXT, CHAPTER 12

Scripture

Be careful for nothing; but in everything by prayer and supplication with thanksgiving let your requests be made known unto God. (Philippians 4:6)

Goal

To help people appreciate the effectiveness of immediately praying for needs without waiting for meetings or a prayer letter.

How to Begin

Begin the meeting with prayer. Here is a sample that might be used, but feel free to pray your own prayer if desired.

Dear Father, thank You that with our modern methods of communication, we can enlist prayer support any time it is needed. Open our hearts to these new technologies, realizing that they are only a quicker means of receiving the needs about which we should pray to You. In Jesus' name, Amen.

Opening Questions

- Share any new method of intercessory prayer you have been able to start or inspire others to begin.
- Report on contacts with some of the non-Christians you are praying for. Are you seeing any results, such as softening of their hearts, interest in Christian things, or someone accepting Jesus?
- Have you finished the book?

Introduction

If there is not a way of obtaining immediate prayer support for yourself, your church members, pastor, or community needs, this session offers a practical solution. "Telephone" prayer chains (including those based on e-mail, text messaging, etc....) are operating successfully in churches and communities all around the world.

Discussion Questions

1. How would a telephone prayer chain among your church members improve communicating and praying for emergencies and needs as they arise in your church?
2. Do you have anyone you feel free to call if a problem, sickness, or emergency arises in your home? How would a telephone prayer chain (in your church, organization, community) help get immediate prayer support for you?
3. Why are telephone prayer chains such an effective way to teach children at home the power of prayer? Could this also be true of your spouse or roommate?

4. What advantages would a telephone prayer chain have over regular prayer meetings, prayer letters mailed to pray-ers, and monthly prayer calendars? How important is it to you to have prayer support immediately when the need arises?

5. As technology increases, how can e-mail, text messaging, websites, social networking, etc. be used for communicating urgent requests? Discuss what advantages and disadvantages these newer communication methods present (availability, cost, etc.).

6. Turn to John 17:22-23 and ask a group member to read it aloud. Consider the unity that could be fostered in your community if a metropolitan prayer chain made up of Christians from many or all of your churches of different denominations were operational. Discuss the values you can see in periodic meetings of all these pray-ers to praise and thank God together for answered prayer.

7. Do you belong to any professional group, school system, or place of employment where the Christians could organize with you and pray for the relationships and personal needs of colleagues—and even for the non-Christians there to find Christ?

8. Discuss a plan for this group to get started organizing and launching a telephone prayer chain. Set a specific time for your first organization meeting. See the end of this study for general instructions and a list of rules for telephone chain members.

9. Bring out prayer books with recorded prayers and answers. Add up the total number of recorded prayer requests during this study and the total for the group

(see Ch. 12, *The Strongest Link*). Multiply those prayers by the number of people in your group who have prayed them and see how many prayers have risen to heaven during this time. Keep this in mind: although you may not have seen the answers yet, God is still working on them, and will answer in His perfect timing and perfect way.

10. Go back to the first prayer promise (James 5:16). Share any ways that you have seen this promise fulfilled in this study time.

Prayer Time

Divide into prayer groups, with a leader directing prayer.

1. Draw close to God, confessing sins if necessary.
2. Listen in silence after the leader asks God to speak to each member about being on a telephone prayer chain.
3. Pray aloud in groups, one at a time, promising God to do whatever He has laid on your heart.
4. Spend time in intercessory prayer using the "six S" method with requests volunteered from members.
5. Leader, close in prayer, thanking God for the privilege the group has had of studying and experiencing new heights in prayer.

Closing Prayer

Thank You, Lord, that You have shown us that "the effectual fervent prayer of a righteous [person] availeth much" (James 5:16). Help us to continue the road to prayer power we have begun. In Jesus' name, Amen.

Assignment

Within the next two weeks, establish a prayer chain organizational group. At the meeting:

1. Study the rules for telephone prayer chains at the end of this chapter.

2. Prayerfully choose a chairperson who is respected by all, who is firm yet loving, who has spiritual insight and wisdom, who knows the difference between praying requests and praying answers, who desires God's will in all political, denominational, and human situations. (God will help develop him or her if you think such a one cannot be found.)

3. Invite others also wanting to pray to be members of your chain. Be sure to train them in prayer power through reading *What Happens When Women Pray*. (This is not just for women!)

4. Have each member sign the Rules for Prayer Chain Members, found at the end of this study.

5. Make sure each chain member records and dates every request and answer.

General Instructions for Telephone Prayer Chains

(Requests are sequentially passed from one member to another in a chain.)

1. A prayer chain should consist of approximately 10 members. The object of prayer chains is to get as many people as possible praying immediately. Divide into as many chains as is necessary. Larger groups can be formed into small chains by having the first few "links" call more than one person.

2. Provide members with a list of names and phone numbers on their chain.

3. Provide members with printed notebook sheets to keep track of prayer requests with date and the answer with date.

4. Have an organizational meeting where each member (1) signs the rules and (2) prays a short prayer of commitment to God, promising Him to call and pray immediately when a request is received.

5. Meet regularly with all members of the prayer chains to pray together and praise God for His answers, thus keeping interest alive and the purpose of the chain clear. Questions can be answered and problems worked out at these meetings.

Rules for Telephone Prayer Chain Members

I. Incoming prayer requests
   A. Prayer requests may come from any source (chain members, those in need of prayer, pastor, church boards, teachers, etc.).
   B. Prayer requests should be phoned to: (chairperson's name, phone number). If no one answers, call: (assistant's name, phone number).
      1. If possible, phone in requests in the morning.
         a) The chairperson will then gather the requests and activate all the morning chains.
         b) The evening chains will be activated that same evening.
         c) Urgent requests may be called in anytime.
   C. Include only the amount of information *you* want communicated.

II. Directions for prayer chain members when receiving a call
   A. Write down the prayer request exactly as dictated to you. (Use the notebook provided to note the request and date requested and the answer and date answered.)
      1. Pass on only the information dictated to you.
      2. Don't distort the information.
      3. Don't gossip about the prayer request during the call.
   B. *Immediately call* the next person on your prayer chain list.
      1. If no one answers, keep calling down the list until someone answers, thus keeping the

chain going. (You may back up later to inform those not answering, but this is not required. If a message was left, the one missing the call should call to receive it. Use mature Christian judgment on what should be left on an answering machine.)

C. Pray immediately concerning requests after making your call.

   1. Don't leave your phone until you have prayed so that you do not become involved in other things and put off praying until it is too late or you forget altogether.

   2. Pray for God's will. (Don't pray answers; pray requests to God.)

   3. Pray fervently. "The effectual fervent prayer of a righteous [person] availeth much" (James 5:16b). You can be the instrument that moves the hand of God.

III. *Use Christian discretion to keep requests confidential.*

IV. *Inform the prayer chairperson when answers are received.* (These too will be passed along to encourage other prayer chain members.)

Signed _____

If at any time you find these rules impossible to follow, please call the chairperson and have your name removed from the prayer chain.

General Instructions for E-Mail Prayer Chains

(Requests are passed from the chair to all members of the chain simultaneously by e-mail, text, etc.)

1. The object of prayer chains is to get as many people as possible praying immediately.
2. Provide members with printed notebook sheets to keep track of prayer requests with date and the answer with date.
3. Have an organizational meeting where each member (1) signs the rules and (2) prays a short prayer of commitment to God, promising Him to pray immediately when a request is received.
4. Meet regularly with all members of the prayer chains to pray together and praise God for His answers, thus keeping interest alive and the purpose of the chain clear. Questions can be answered and problems worked out at these meetings.

Rules for E-mail Prayer Chain Members

I. Incoming prayer requests

    A. Prayer requests may come from any source (chain members, those in need of prayer, pastor, church boards, teachers, etc.).

    B. Prayer requests should be phoned or e-mailed to: (chairperson's name, phone number, e-mail). If no one answers, contact: (assistant's name, phone number, e-mail). The person requesting prayer should email a copy of the request to the assistant chair.

Note that e-mails can often be read by other members of the household, including children. Be particularly aware of the content of e-mailed prayer requests. Sensitive requests should be worded subtly (God knows the details) with any necessary details communicated by phone.

        1. If possible, e-mail requests in the morning.

            a) The chairperson will then gather the requests and activate all the morning chains.

            b) The evening chains will be activated that same evening.

            c) Urgent requests may be communicated anytime.

    C. Include only the amount of information *you* want communicated.

II. Directions for prayer chain members when receiving an e-mail or text message

    A. Save the e-mail or write down the prayer requests exactly as included in the e-mail. (Use the

notebook provided to note the request and date requested and the answer and date answered.)
B. Pray immediately concerning requests.
  1. Don't leave your computer until you have prayed so that you do not become involved in other things and put off praying until it is too late or you forget altogether.
  2. Pray for God's will. (Don't pray answers; pray requests to God.)
  3. Pray fervently. "The effectual fervent prayer of a righteous [person] availeth much" (James 5:16b). You can be the instrument that moves the hand of God.

III. *Use Christian discretion to keep requests confidential.*

IV. *Inform the prayer chairperson when answers are received.* (These too will be passed along to encourage other prayer chain members.)

Signed _____

If at any time you find these rules impossible to follow, please call the chairperson and have your name removed from the prayer chain.

CPSIA information can be obtained
at www.ICGtesting.com
Printed in the USA
BVHW052026060722
641447BV00003B/583

9 780981 746784